World War I: The "Great War"
Part I

Professor Vejas Gabriel Liulevicius

THE TEACHING COMPANY ®

PUBLISHED BY:

THE TEACHING COMPANY
4151 Lafayette Center Drive, Suite 100
Chantilly, Virginia 20151-1232
1-800-TEACH-12
Fax—703-378-3819
www.teach12.com

ISBN 1-59803-154-6

Vejas Gabriel Liulevicius, Ph.D.
Associate Professor of History, University of Tennessee

Vejas Gabriel Liulevicius was born in Chicago, Illinois. He grew up on Chicago's Southside in a Lithuanian-American neighborhood and also spent some years attending school in Aarhus, Denmark, and Bonn, Germany. He received his B.A. from the University of Chicago. In 1989, he spent the summer in Moscow and Leningrad (today St. Petersburg) in intensive language study in Russian. He earned his Ph.D. from the University of Pennsylvania in European history in 1994, specializing in modern German history.

After receiving his doctorate, Professor Liulevicius spent a year as a postdoctoral research fellow at the Hoover Institution on War, Peace, and Revolution at Stanford University in Palo Alto, California. Since 1995, he has been a history professor at the University of Tennessee in Knoxville and holds the Hendrickson Professorship in the College of Arts and Sciences for 2005–2007. He teaches courses on modern German history, Western civilization, Nazi Germany, World War I, war and culture, 20th-century Europe, nationalism, and utopian thought. In 2003, he received the University of Tennessee's Excellence in Teaching Award. In 2005, he was awarded a National Endowment for the Humanities Fellowship for his research.

Professor Liulevicius's research focuses on German relations with Eastern Europe in the modern period. His other interests include the utopian tradition and its impact on modern politics, images of the United States abroad, and the history of the Baltic region. He has published numerous articles, and his first book, *War Land on the Eastern Front: Culture, National Identity and German Occupation in the First World War* (2000, Cambridge University Press), also appeared in German translation in 2002. His next book project is a larger study of German stereotypes of Eastern Europeans and ideas of a special German cultural mission in the East over the last two centuries, entitled *The German Myth of the East*.

Professor Liulevicius also has recorded another course with The Teaching Company, *Utopia and Terror in the 20th Century*. He lives in Knoxville, Tennessee, with his wife, Kathleen, and their son, Paul.

Table of Contents
World War I: The "Great War"
Part I

World War I: The "Great War"

Scope:

The First World War came as a dreadful surprise to those who experienced it, due to its magnitude, global expanse, unprecedented violence, and shattering impact on Western civilization. This course of 36 lectures explores the continuous series of brutal surprises and shocks that the first example of a "total war" brought, a conflict not limited to armies, but pitting entire societies against each other in mortal struggle. An estimated 70 million men were mobilized and approximately 9 million died. The civilizational impact of an industrial slaughter on this scale was so significant that World War I set the 20th century on its violent course, culminating in a later, perfected total war, World War II.

We combine chronological and thematic approaches for an in-depth look at this conflict's many dimensions, integrating military history with social, political, intellectual, and cultural history. Unlike narratives of World War I that emphasize the Western Front with scant attention to other theaters, this course provides comprehensive coverage of all fronts. Likewise, we consider not only political elites and generals but also the lives of ordinary soldiers and civilians. Major themes include the surprising eagerness to plunge into mutual slaughter; the unexpected endurance of societies undergoing this ordeal; the radically different hopes and hatreds that war evoked, with remarkable contrasts in Western and Eastern Europe; and the way in which the Great War functioned as a hinge of violence, opening the door to the normalization of previously unsuspected levels of violence, including against civilians, a dynamic that hurried Europe toward renewed conflict.

Our first six lectures depict the state of Europe and the world as the 1914 cataclysm approached and then struck. We examine internal politics of the Great Powers and growing tensions among them, reacting to the expansion of German power, as well as important currents of thought (both optimistic and pessimistic) in intellectual life. We examine the slide into the abyss: origins of the July crisis, beginning with an act of terrorism in Sarajevo; historians' debates on the war's true causes and where the main responsibility lies; the striking "August Madness" celebrations; and the breakdown of longstanding military plans for short, decisive war.

The next three lectures—Seven through Nine—cover the Western Front and the surreal trench landscape that emerged there. We examine technological reasons for the stalemate that the trenches represented, desperate and costly attempts to break it, strange patterns of death and life (including tacit truces) developed by ordinary soldiers, and vain and horrific battles at Verdun, the Somme, and Ypres. Lectures Ten and Eleven cover lesser known theaters: the vast, open Eastern Front where Germans battered Russia, even as final victory eluded them, and the Southern Front, including the Alps, the Balkans, and the doomed Allied Gallipoli expedition against Ottoman Turkey.

Lectures Twelve through Fifteen take a closer look at particularly important themes. We survey combatant countries' war aims and the experience of foreign occupation. The suffering of ordinary soldiers is confronted, as we discuss military medicine, psychological traumas, and the experience of 8 million prisoners of war. Although many men broke down under the strain of combat, others exulted in it: elite storm troopers were among them, as well as two men, Benito Mussolini and Adolf Hitler, who later became dictators as they sought to recreate wartime experience. This section concludes by investigating rapidly changing technology, as machine guns, poison gas, and tanks were deployed to mass-produce death ever more efficiently.

The next three lectures—Sixteen through Eighteen—return our attention to other theaters: war in the air and at sea and surprises and confounded expectations in each. The war's global reach, its colonial dimension, and the attempt to win sympathy in world opinion are examined in detail.

Our next set of lectures concerns internal home-front politics. In comparative fashion, we note similarities as well as striking differences in how nations reacted. Lectures Nineteen to Twenty-Three reveal centralized state control of economies, societies, and propaganda to create martial enthusiasm. We cover the privations and extraordinary endurance of many societies, as well as growing signs of stress and breakdown, to understand civilian experience. New social divisions arose, threatening cohesion. Dissent could be explosive, and we explore protest and its growth or suppression. By the later years of the war, 1916–1917, a fresh remobilization of energies was needed to continue fighting.

The next five lectures cover dramatic new departures in world history created by total war. The 1915 slaughter of Armenians in the Ottoman Empire launched a series of 20th-century genocides. War's strains encouraged revolts, socialist and nationalist, radically reenvisaging the political future. In the Russian Empire, turbulent events produced the first attempt at total revolution, launching the Soviet Union's communist experiment. America's 1917 entry into the war announced a new, expansive role for the United States in world affairs, while its society was convulsed by mobilization for intervention overseas.

Lectures Twenty-Nine through Thirty-Three cover the war's immediate outcome. After the failure of Germany's last gamble and defeat, the November 11, 1918, Armistice closed the war, even as aftershocks continued: the unprecedented collapse of the German, Austro-Hungarian, and Turkish Empires, and the onset of ideological warfare among nationalists, revolutionaries, and counterrevolutionaries, in an atmosphere of European civil war. We analyze the 1919 peace settlement in Paris and the Versailles Treaty.

The last three lectures examine the war's deeper impact on Western civilization. Drawing on rich, recent scholarship in cultural history, we follow the war's echoes (and anguished questions of what it had ultimately meant) in monuments, collective rituals of commemoration, literature and art, and also in poisonous myths and conspiracy theories concerning the war. Most ominously, new and fierce ideological mass movements—spearheaded by Fascists, Nazis, and Communists—were so inspired by the experience of total war that they aimed to restructure politics along military lines and achieve permanent mobilization of state and society. Ultimately, our course concludes with a summation of the Great War's effects, its implications for the rest of the century, and the new world that it created.

Lecture One

The Century's Initial Catastrophe

Scope:

This lecture presents the main themes of the course, beginning with the crucial concept of "Total War," with the First World War considered the first example of this modern phenomenon. Total war is not merely a contest between professional armies, but rather represents a clash of entire societies mobilized for total victory, including their economies, political establishments, and intellectual life. Other important themes include the roles that ideology and fervent beliefs had in the war's course and conduct, the meanings that were ascribed to the war while it was going on and in its aftermath (with great contrasts in Western and Eastern Europe), the shock of new experiences and brutalization, and the implications of the Great War for our civilization and our own times.

Outline

I. Envisioning the War

    A. From the distance of nearly a century, it is both difficult and compelling to seek to envision the reality of what contemporaries called "The Great War," in part because the war did so much to shape our modern world.

    B. One way to begin envisioning the experience of the war is to consider the mixed scenes that accompanied its start and its end.

        1. In 1914, the war began with vast, cheering crowds, in an event called the August Madness. Yet there were also quiet leave-takings and individual foreboding.

        2. In 1918, as the guns fell silent, unnatural stillness reigned over the cemeteries and battlefields. Yet elsewhere, especially in Eastern Europe, national rebirth and independence were celebrated.

    C. It is also difficult to take in the magnitude of the war's scale.

        1. Mass armies were mobilized, with an estimated 70 million soldiers participating in the war worldwide, of whom more than 9 million would be killed.

2. This number works out to 6,000 soldiers dying for every day of the war.

3. The precise number of deaths and casualties will likely never be known with precision.

4. Civilian casualties also remain unclear, but some estimates run to 5.95 million.

D. Even the term *World War* was unique.

1. Although earlier wars had had global dimensions, the term "world war" was used to signify the extraordinary reach of this unprecedented conflict.

2. The extent of 19th-century imperialism spread the conflict around the globe.

II. Aims of the Course

A. This course combines a thematic approach with chronological coverage.

B. It surveys cultural, social, and political as well as military history and presents a narrative balanced among all fronts rather than focused almost exclusively on the more familiar Western Front.

III. Main Themes of the Course

A. The Totality of War: Defining *Total War* as a Concept

1. *Total war* was a term coined during the war itself to sum up the all-encompassing nature of this modern industrial conflict.

2. It demanded total mobilization of mass armies, economies, societies, and the hearts and minds of people in the countries at war. In this sense, it was a people's war, not one determined by government cabinets and elites.

3. Increasingly, the stakes of total war were seen as total as well: victory or sheer defeat would be the final outcome, not compromise. The winner would be the last one standing after the drawn-out process of attrition.

4. Total war had other important implications.

    a. Because civilians were mobilized to work for their country's victory on the "home front," civilians were increasingly targets of violence as well.

    b. Total war had a crucial economic dimension, as victory would not be found on the battlefield alone. Thus economic blockades (like the British naval blockade of Germany) were an obvious tool used to deny the enemy resources.

    c. The enormous demands and strains of total war tore at societies.

    d. Gaps could grow between the soldiers in the trenches, the civilians on the home front, and the governments seeking to fight the war. Social tensions often led to the search for scapegoats in one's own midst.

5. Though the term *total war* was new, it came into its own after the war, as participants thought out the implications of what they had lived through. Unfortunately, the term became important in planning for the next war, World War II.

6. The experience of total war affected movements arising out of the ruins of the conflict. These movements were called "totalitarian" because of their total claims: Communism in Russia, Fascism in Italy, and Nazism in Germany.

7. Their ambitions were to produce completely mobilized societies, building on the lived reality of the Great War.

B. The Neglected Role of Ideology

1. World War I has often been depicted as a conflict over geopolitics and the balance of power, as opposed to World War II, which is seen as much more ideological.

2. In fact, ideas and beliefs played a crucial role throughout World War I and need to be understood.

3. Some historians in fact urge us to conceptualize a distinct "war culture" that developed over the course of the conflict. The eagerness that the war elicited was afterwards willfully forgotten.

4. Given such hopes and emotions from the very beginning, what changes followed?

C. "Meanings" of the War

    1. How was war understood by those who participated in it and remembered it afterwards?

    2. It is crucial to acknowledge that in the experience of contemporaries, there was a multiplicity of wars. For instance, war on the Western Front and the Eastern Front could be distinctly different.

    3. Western memory of the Great War focuses on senseless sacrifice.

    4. In Eastern Europe's newly independent states, by contrast, the Great War was seen as a purposeful event, producing national independence.

    5. Likewise, in a related paradoxical reversal, whereas World War II is regarded as "the good war" in the West, the perspective in Eastern Europe is more ambivalent.

D. The Shock of the New and Brutalization

    1. The war presented many novelties that, unfortunately, later became increasingly ordinary.

    2. These novelties included new weapons, such as tanks, airplanes, and poison gas; new approaches to war that targeted civilians; genocide (the Armenian massacres); and new powers for the state and strategies for the "population policy."

    3. Though extremely difficult to measure, contemporaries felt that a process of brutalization had taken place, hardening sensibilities and altering the value of human life. The war functioned as a hinge of violence in modern history.

E. Implications of the Great War

    1. World War I has left its mark on us in this day in ways both small and large.

    2. Its traces are in our language (in such words and phrases as *trenches, No Man's Land, going over the top*); in mundane objects, including wristwatches and trench coats; and in Daylight Savings Time.

    3. On the most significant level, the war led to changes in the status of the state, society, and the individual.

4. Paradoxically, the "disillusionment" of the war also produced fierce ideological politics that led to a new "Age of Belief," with ideological choices brooking no neutrality, and culminating in World War II. (The link between the war and its political aftermath is made clear by figures whom we will encounter here and who later played roles in World War II: Winston Churchill, Charles de Gaulle, Adolf Hitler, Benito Mussolini, and others.)

5. The war seemingly normalized a massive brutalization of the civilization.

6. The American diplomat and historian George Kennan called it the "seminal catastrophe" of 20th century.

7. In many ways, it has shaped the world we know today: its borders, its perils, nightmares, and hopes.

IV. Overview of Individual Lectures

    A. The first six lectures depict the state of Europe and the world in 1914 as the war approached.

        1. We will examine the Great Powers and the growing tensions among them.

        2. We will explore the causes of the war and the ultimate breakdown of plans for a short, decisive war.

    B. Lectures Seven through Nine examine the Western Front and the horrors of trench warfare.

    C. Lectures Ten and Eleven cover the Eastern and Southern Fronts, lesser-known but still important theaters.

    D. Lectures Twelve through Fifteen look at various aspects of the war.

        1. We will study the war aims of various combatant countries and the experience of foreign occupation.

        2. We will look at the psychological and medical suffering of ordinary soldiers and the experience of prisoners of war.

        3. We will consider the phenomenon of those who exulted in war.

        4. We will investigate the technological advances that affected the war, not always for the better.

E. Lectures Sixteen through Eighteen cover the war in the air, at sea, and around the globe.

F. Lectures Nineteen through Twenty-Three concern internal politics.

    1. We will look at how different nations reacted to the war.

    2. We will examine the effects of propaganda, privation, and stress on the civilian populations of those nations.

    3. We also study dissent within those countries and the effort to remobilize in the last years of the war.

G. Lectures Twenty-Four through Twenty-Eight examine dramatic departures in world history brought about by the war.

    1. We will cover the Armenian massacres, revolts, and revolutions.

    2. We will also consider the entry of the United States into the war and how our participation affected life in America and the outcome of the war.

H. Lectures Twenty-Nine through Thirty-Three cover the war's outcome and aftershocks worldwide.

I. The last three lectures look at the deeper and lasting impact of the war on Western civilization.

Essential Reading:

John Keegan, *The First World War*.

A. J. P. Taylor, *The First World War: An Illustrated History*.

Supplementary Reading:

Modris Eksteins, *Rites of Spring: The Great War and the Birth of the Modern Age*.

Questions to Consider:

1. Is it possible to measure the brutalization of a civilization? If so, what criteria would track that process?

2. Is *total war* the best concept to define the two world wars of the 20th century?

Lecture One—Transcript
The Century's Initial Catastrophe

Welcome to this course on the First World War, the manmade catastrophe that launched the 20th century on its violent course and indeed a key event of modern times. In this lecture, we will begin by presenting the main themes of the course beginning with the crucial concept of "Total War," as many historians consider the First World War the first example of this modern phenomenon.

"Total War" is a phrase used to describe not merely a contest between professional armies on the battlefield, but rather represents something far vaster, a clash in entire societies mobilized for total victory including their economies, their political establishments, their intellectual life of a society, all of the passions and feeling, emotions and convictions of an entire population.

Our other important themes will include the role that ideology and fervent beliefs had in determining the war's course and its conduct. Also, the meanings that were ascribed to the war as it was going on, as well as in its aftermath, and we'll examine here great contrasts in how the war was understood, as well, the shock of new experiences, a continual process of the shock of the new, and a process, a steady process of brutalization, and finally the implications of this Great War for our civilization and for our own times.

It's necessary thus to engage in a very difficult, but nonetheless essential task of historical imagination, to seek to envision the war in its totality. This is in many ways a very difficult task that faces us. We're removed from the war by a distance of nearly a century; the war itself to contemporaries was of such a scale and of such novelty that they called it, "The Great War" to express something of its all-encompassing nature. And then finally, another reason why it's difficult for us to envision the war in its totality is because that war has done so much to shape our modern world, as we'll see in coming lectures.

One way however to begin the task of envisioning the experience of the war is to consider bookend scenes of that conflict; scenes accompanying its start, as well as its end that say much to us about the mixed nature of experiences in the First World War, some of its ambiguities and its diversity.

In August of 1914, the war began. And it did so with a break at long last to the tension that had gripped many Europeans. In August of 1914 with the Declarations of War, that tension at last broke and a remarkable emotional reaction set in. Vast cheering crowds throughout the capitals of Europe welcomed the war. In London, in Paris, in Berlin, and in St. Petersburg, crowds gathered to sing national anthems, to wave national flags, to cheer and to volunteer for the conflict.

This event, this emotional reaction, came to be called "The August Madness," and for many was an unforgettable experience. At the same time as you had these vast celebrations however, there were also contrary phenomena; quiet leave takings, as soldiers left for the front, well aware that they might not return; individual foreboding, for not everyone cheered, not everyone celebrated. Many understood the suffering that war would bring, if not ultimately its scale. And then finally there's also the case of ethnic minorities in the multinational empires of Europe. The Poles for instance, divided between three empires who well understood that it was not their national cause that they would be asked to sacrifice and die for, but rather that of a foreign regime.

At the end of the war four year's later, in November of 1918, as the guns last fell silent, as opposed to the tremendous celebration of four year's previously, now quiet reigned. An unnatural stillness settled on the cemeteries and the battlefields that had been the site of the suffering of four years previous. At the same time however in a contrary phenomenon elsewhere in Europe, especially in Eastern Europe, there emerged new nations from the wreckage of empire, and crowds celebrated there the message of national rebirth and independence.

These scenes bookending the conflict, suggest something of its diversity and its complexity. Another challenge for us is to try to even take in the magnitude of the war scale, one of the reasons why contemporaries called it the Great War. Mass armies were mobilized on a scale that simply had been unimaginable hitherto. An estimated 70 million soldiers participated in the war worldwide; and of them, over 9 million would be killed.

To give some sense of this otherwise astronomical figure, one might mention that on average, this works out to about 6,000 soldiers dying for every day of the war as it took its course. At the same time, we need to mention that even these astronomical figures lack a total precision, the precise number of deaths and casualties will likely never be known exactly given the disorder and the lack of certainty about these figures that dominated the end of the conflict. Another question which historians are still debating today is that of civilian casualties. Those numbers are not clear, but some estimates run to almost 6 million.

A further key aspect of this war that we need to try to assimilate or take aboard is its identity as a World War. "World War" was a term used at the time as well to express the magnitude of this Great War. Contemporaries obviously were not yet calling it the First World War; even the most pessimistic couldn't expect that this would be the first in a series of conflicts.

Nonetheless, the concept itself took on an important dimension. Earlier war, such as the Seven Year War of the 18th century, or the Napoleonic War of the early 19th century, had had a global dimension, but in some sense, this war had an even more extended global aspect. And one reason for this was the extent of 19th century imperialism spreading the conflict around the globe.

If our largest undertaking in this course is to try to take in some of the reality of this conflict in its totality, we want also to outline some of the aims of the course as we proceed. We'll be presenting, not only a chronological narrative—and we certainly will be doing that, as well—we'll also be combining this with a thematic approach, taking a moment now and again to really focus in on particular themes and topics of crucial importance. At the same time as we'll be covering military history, we'll also be seeking to include in our survey cultural, social and political aspects of the conflict, as well. We'll also be trying to present a narrative that's balanced between the different war fronts, rather than being, as is sometimes the case, almost exclusively focused on the more familiar and riveting scenes of the Western Front.

We need now to outline some of the main themes of the course, and these are essentially five. The first one concerns the totality of war, defining "Total War" as a concept. "Total War" was a term that was coined and used during the war itself in an attempt to sum up what contemporaries felt was the all encompassing nature of this modern industrial conflict. This new kind of war demanded total mobilization of mass armies, economies, and societies in the hearts and minds of people in the war, not merely soldiers on the battlefield. In this sense, this was not merely a war determined by government cabinets and elites, but in a very real sense, a people's war.

And certain implications flowed from the totality of this new conflict. Increasingly, the stakes of Total War were seen as "total," as well. Not merely an adjustment of competitive advantage as a result of battles or of territorial loss or gain, but total victory or total defeat would become the final outcome, not compromise. This long grinding process of Total War also would not bring quick victory, but the winner in fact would be the last one standing after a long drawn-out process of attrition.

Total War had other important implications as well, because not only soldiers were involved, but also civilians. Civilians took on a new importance. They too were mobilized to work for their country's victory on what came to be called the "home front." This is a marvelously expressive phrase that really captures a key aspect of Total War. And as a result of this new importance, civilians were increasingly the targets of violence, as well.

Very clearly, Total War as a modern industrial conflict would also have a crucial economic dimension, as victory would not be found on the battlefield alone. And thus, economic weapons—like the naval blockade of the British of Germany, to deny enemy resources—were obvious tools. The enormous demands and strains of this phenomenon of Total War would also tear at all the societies engaged in the conflict. And these strains in society could take many different forms. Gaps could grow between the soldiers in the trenches and civilians; and on the home front, with incomprehension growing between these parties and alienation from the government seeking to fight the war to a successful conclusion, all too often social tensions could also lead to the search for scapegoats and minorities in ones own midst.

Now though the term "Total War" was new and was used during the First World War itself, it actually really came into its own in popular usage after the war. As participants, contemporaries who had survived the conflict, tried to think out the implications of what they had lived through. And it's unfortunately a fact that the concept of

Total War in part came into its own because it was used by those who were already thinking about the next war and preparing for it, World War II.

The experience of total war also affected political movements that in a sense arose out of the ruins of that conflict. These radical political movements were often called "totalitarian" because of their total claims upon people and societies. These included Communism in Soviet Russia, Fascism in Italy, and Nazism in Hitler's Germany. The ambitions of these movements, however different their ideologies were, were often rooted in the experience of the Great War. Their aims were to produce completely mobilized societies acting in unison and in ideological struggle.

The second major theme that we'll be returning to over the course of this course is the neglected role of ideology. The First World War has often been depicted by historians as a conflict over geopolitics, the balance of power and political issues, as opposed to the Second World War, which is seen as much more ideological, a complicated contest between democracies, Nazism and the Soviet Union. In fact, this juxtaposition is overdrawn. Ideas and beliefs clearly played a crucial role throughout World War I and need to be understood.

Some historians today are stressing this in their scholarship. They're urging us to conceptualize the context of the First World War as a distinct "war culture," which developed over the course of the conflict and which had a very serious ideological dimension. The eagerness with which the war was met, the eagerness which the war elicited was afterwards, they argue, willfully forgotten in a narrative of disillusionment. Given such hopes and emotions from the very beginning of the war, what changes might follow?

Our next major theme is that of the meanings assigned to the war. How was the war understood by those who participated in it and remembered it afterwards? It's crucial to acknowledge one central point. In the experience of contemporaries, we might say that there wasn't merely one First World War, but rather a multiplicity of wars, and this is something we'll be returning to in our lectures. The war on the Western Front was very different from that of the Eastern Front or the other fronts. And thus, all of these different experiences need to be taken into account.

Western memory of the Great War is very different from that is dominant in Eastern Europe in the 20th century. The memory of Western Europeans of the Great War tended to focus, in the decades after that conflict, on senseless sacrifice, on the bloody extinction of an entire generation of youth, for what? By contrast, a very different set of meaning were assigned to the Great War in Eastern Europe in its aftermath. In newly independent nation-states by contrast in Eastern Europe, the Great War was seen not as senseless or meaningless, but instead as the very exemplar of a purposeful event producing national independence in a baptism of fire.

And likewise, in a related and paradoxical reversal, some of these contrasts reverberate later in the 20th century. In Western Europe, World War II is often regarded as "the good war." The perspective in Eastern Europe on the Second World War is much more ambivalent. By contrast, their Nazi rule was replaced by decades of Communist control, and the narrative is not simply one of liberation.

The next major theme is the process of repeated shocks of new experiences that needed to be assimilated or taken aboard, culminating in an overall and prolonged process of brutalization. The war presented an unceasing series of novelties that unfortunately later became increasingly ordinary and feature in our own times. These included the use of vast new technologically sophisticated weapon systems, including tanks, airplanes, as well as that dreadful weapon, poison gas. These included new approaches to war that targeted civilians. They included also the devastating modern phenomenon of genocide, including the Armenian massacres in the Ottoman Empire that we'll be discussing in a later lecture.

It also expanded the powers of the state and created new strategies for dealing with populations in what came to be called "population policy." Ultimately, though extremely difficult to measure, many contemporaries, especially the more sensitive and thoughtful ones, felt that they were living through a process of brutalization, in which the sensibilities of ordinary individuals, as well as societies, were in a sense hardening. And the value of human life was being altered and downgraded. The war thus functioned as a hinge of violence in modern history, preparing greater horrors to come.

Out last major theme of the course are the implications of the Great War in the largest sense. Because the First World War has left its mark on us in this day in ways both small as well as large, its traces indeed are to be found in our language today. These include phrases that we utter perhaps in the workplace about "going into the trenches" or "fighting, slogging it out in the trenches." Another phrase is that of a "No-Man's Land," which crops up in our everyday language as well, which originally designated those territories located between the trench lines, which represented the central area of combat. And then a phrase also harkening back to the First World War, the phrase, "going over the top," which represented in fact the notion of a frontal attack of troops leaping up out of the trenches, heading out across No-Man's Land in order to engage in, it was hoped, a victorious assault on the enemy side. These are traces left in our language.

Other objects that to us are quite ordinary also are rooted in the experience of the First World War. These included mundane objects like wristwatches. Indeed, in the 19th century, a proper gentleman would wear a pocket watch rather than a wristwatch. But in the trenches of the First World War, the use of wristwatches in order to readily coordinate attacks going over the top at a precisely predetermined and planned time produced the popularity of the wristwatch replacing pocket watches. Even trench coats still worn today are very much artifacts of that time and that place.

An ordinary phenomenon that we experience twice a year, that of Daylight Saving's Time, the transition in how we lead our lives on an ordinary schedule, harkens back to the First World War, as in nations mobilizing for total conflict, the state would determine when it was necessary to change our experience of time itself in order to prolong the working day.

At the most significant level, the war also led to changes of a really profound nature in the status of the state, that's to say the government, and the powers that it was willing to claim and that individuals were willing to accept as claims. Status of society changed as well, and the calls that it could make on individuals. And then also the status of the individual himself or herself changed as a result of this vast conflict as well.

Indeed, some historians have argued on a very profound level that even our language changed. And we'll be discussing in later lectures this remarkable and provocative thesis that the English language itself, among others, changed in the way certain words operated. The argument gets made that after the searing disillusionment of the First World War, the words "honor" and "duty" for instance could never be spoken again without an element of irony. This is a claim that we'll be examining in a later lecture.

At the same time, paradoxically, one of the outcomes of the First World War and even of this alleged process of "disillusionment" was not a loss of faith, but a renewed and even more explosive political faith, the production of fierce new ideological politics in a new age of belief. The decades that followed the First World War were ones of extreme politics, with ideological choices in which individuals who were not afforded the right to any kind of neutrality, but instead would have to make choices between opposed ideologies.

The growth of this extremism across the political spectrum ultimately culminated in a repetition of the phenomenon of Total War in the Second World War. And the linkages between these two global conflicts are made clear in a very ordinary way in some of the figures whom we'll encounter in the course of our lectures who played roles in both the First World War and later in the Second World War. These include the British politician and later leader, Winston Churchill. They include the young officer during the First World War, Charles de Gaulle, who had later rallied the French resistance cause. They include an ordinary soldier who had later become the dictator of Nazi Germany, Adolf Hitler, as well as another future dictator, Benito Mussolini, and many others.

The linkages between these two World Wars are such that historians have begun to provocatively suggest that it may very well be that we need to think not only of separate conflicts, but rather of an extended continuum of conflict of clash that we might need to think about as a Thirty Years War of the 20th century, rather than as distinct conflicts. And it's likely to be the case that as we recede in time from the experience of both World Wars, from the perspective of those who come later, these events will draw closer and closer, and the perspective will be altered for people in the future.

What was clearly recognized by contemporaries was that the First World War, and then later the Second World War, seemingly normalized a massive brutalization of our shared civilization. In a famous phrase still echoed by historians as nearly obligatory, the American diplomat and historian, George Kennan, described the

First World War as the "seminal catastrophe" of 20th century. And what he meant by that was that the First World War had unleashed a whole series of processes and dynamics that ultimately would set the 20th century on its destructive course. In many ways, as we'll be exploring in our course, the First World War has shaped the world we know today; many of its political borders; its regional conflicts; many of the perils, nightmares and hopes that are with us still.

We'd like to briefly provide an overview of the individual lectures to see the trajectory that our course will be taking. In our first six lectures, we will be examining the outbreak of the war after having provided an overview of the context in which Europe and the world found itself in 1914 and immediately before. We will have examined the crisis in politics and culture. We'll examine a still very lively debate about the causes of the war and we'll take a much closer look at this riveting mass psychological phenomenon of the August Madness of 1914, immediately before an unexpected breakdown in the war plans, which were to bring, it was hoped, a quick victory to the fighting sides.

In our following three lectures, we'll examine the Western Front, which has such an iconic and clearly very important status as a site of modernity for our own times. We'll examine the experience of what it was like to live and die in the trenches. We'll examine the titanic battles that were fought on the Western Front and which brought so little in terms of victory. We'll then shift our attention to view other fronts and other dimensions of the war's experience. We'll examine what has been called the "unknown war" on the Eastern Front. We'll examine the Southern Fronts and the Mediterranean as another crucial area of operations.

Our course then will turn in our next four lectures, for an extended and careful look at particular themes that span the fighting fronts as well as chronological scope. We'll examine the war aims of the fighting powers, what it was that they were willing to state that they were fighting for. We'll also examine the experience bound up in war aims of occupations and its attempts to seize territory. We'll examine as well soldiers in their identity not merely as fighters, but also as victims, and the dimensions of violence in the battlefield, what it meant physically, as well as the experience that many soldiers shared in of captivity of being prisoners. We'll examine reactions to the war and its experience at the battlefront in the form of "storm troopers," soldiers who exulted in the experience of war and future dictators, Hitler and Mussolini. We then will examine also the Total War of technology, and trace a remarkable process of ever accelerating advances in technological change, with ever more destructive potential realized.

Our next lectures will turn to examine other theaters of the war, the war in the air and the war at sea, as well as a lecture devoted entirely to the global reach and the scope of the war. Our next five lectures then will turn to examine the experience of the war at home, what it meant for governments, societies, and individuals as they mobilized for the conflict itself. We'll examine the invention of the wartime state, as vast new powers accrued to governments mobilizing populations and economies for all-out victory. We'll examine the remarkable and increasing sophistication of propaganda, the attempt to motivate societies' hearts and minds for endurance as well as victory in the war.

We'll then examine more closely the experience of endurance and the stress that was very much a part of the experience of the home fronts. We'll examine the possibilities for dissent against the war and the limits placed upon it. And then in a special lecture, we'll look more closely at the remarkable challenge that essentially the midpoint of the war represented in terms of a renewed tensing of energies and a mustering of will to continue, the fight from 1916–17 on.

Our next lectures will be devoted then to examining some of the destructive consequences of the strains of Total War. We'll devote a lecture to look more closely at how the First World War provided the context for an act of modern genocide, the massacres against the Armenians in 1915, in the Ottoman Empire. A program of population policy tipped over into genocide, that's to say the killing of a group of people not because of what they had done, but rather because of whom they are and what they represent to those committing this crime. We'll examine also the plethora of social and national revolts that erupted as a result of the strains of war, especially felt keenly by multinational empires unable to mobilize effectively for the conflict itself.

Our next lectures then will turn to two world historical events that take place in 1917, and that truly—as we've already suggested earlier in this lecture—in some sense reverberate through the rest of the 20th century. In 1917, the Russian revolutions break out and the United States enters the war with remarkable and important results. We'll examine the complicated course of revolutionary events within Russia itself in 1917, with successive changes of revolutionary regimes culminating in the coming to power of Lenin and the Bolsheviks announcing a "new world order" on the lines of their Communist ideology.

We'll also examine the other paired world historical event of 1917, America's entry into the war, also, with an announced ideological goal of reshaping the world order; and with a very keen and important ideological charge. We'll examine in detail not only the reasons for America's entry into the war, but also the experience of Americans in the war over there, across the Atlantic, as well as in wartime America at home.

We'll then examine the remarkable and quick series of events in 1918, which brought an end to the wartime efforts of the Central Powers—Germany, Austria-Hungary and Turkey. We will examine the emotions that attended the ending of the war in 1918, the collapse of empires with remarkable rapidity, and the achievement of national independence by many independent states in Eastern Europe.

We will bring out course to a close by examining attempts as peacemaking; in particular, the Versailles Treaty and the Paris Settlement, as well as the aftershocks that followed the war, which didn't have a neat end, but instead continued in a very real sense for years afterwards.

We'll examine also the echoes of the war in the form of monuments, memory, and myth, as well as conspiracy theories about the war and its meaning. And, as a result of the tremendous experiences and devastation of the First World War, the beginning of the rise of mass dictatorships, which would have everything to do with the unleashing of the Second World War.

In our very last lecture, we'll examine the legacies of the Great War and indicate not only how it changed the course of modern history, but how it continues to affect us to this very day.

Lecture Two
Europe in 1914

Scope:

This lecture sets the stage for the explosion of the war in 1914 by examining the state of Europe and the world before the cataclysm. We survey the nation-states considered Great Powers (Great Britain, France, Germany, Austria-Hungary, and Russia) and other contenders for Great Power status. We examine the diplomatic history of their dynamic interaction, summed up in the concept of the Balance of Power, and the changes that the emergence of the German Empire caused in the international system. Worldwide imperialism, the growing arms race on land and at sea, and increasing international tensions moved Europe, after a century of general peace, toward a general war.

Outline

I. European Society and the New 20th Century

    A. At the start of the century, European countries were part of a self-confident civilization.

    B. Organized into separate nation-states and empires, Europeans nonetheless in many ways shared a common worldview.

    C. Within Western civilization, some states (known as Great Powers) played dominant roles in international affairs, whereas other states aspired to such a role.

II. The Great Powers

    A. Great Britain

        1. An industrial and commercial power that had spearheaded the Industrial Revolution, Britain also possessed a world empire that encompassed 20 percent of the world's land mass.

        2. Britain's own population was 45 million.

        3. Dependent on trade, it had made itself the preeminent naval power and preferred to maintain "splendid isolation" from the affairs of the European continent.

4. A constitutional monarchy, Britain had a liberal government.

5. London was the banking capital of the world.

B. Germany

1. Imperial Germany had been created by war in 1870–1871, when the German kingdom of Prussia had led German armies to victory against France.

2. The "Iron Chancellor" Otto von Bismarck, peerless practitioner of *Realpolitik* (power politics), had engineered German unification around the hard Prussian militarist core by wars against Austria (1866) and against France.

3. Germany became the strongest power on the continent, with proud Prussian militarist traditions. Its population was 65 million, while its booming economy likewise made it a powerhouse.

4. The creation of the German Empire was of such importance to international affairs that it was called the "German Revolution." The related "German Question" concerned what role Germany would play in European affairs: Would it be a source of stability or instability?

5. Bismarck pursued policies that aimed to reassure the other Great Powers of Germany's peaceful intentions.

6. When the young Kaiser Wilhelm II of the House of Hohenzollern ascended to the throne in 1888, he soon dismissed Bismarck in 1890.

7. Determined to win respect and status for Germany, Wilhelm II sanctioned an aggressive foreign policy that shortly alienated many powers.

8. Though it had a parliament called the *Reichstag*, the empire was an uneasy mix of constitutionalism and authoritarianism.

9. German domestic politics were fragmented along class, regional, and religious lines.

10. Rapid and late industrialization, however, would also bring social disruption.

11. A new political force was the S.P.D., the Social Democratic Party of Germany. Founded in 1875, the S.P.D. adhered to Marxist ideas and was so well organized that it was a model for other socialists worldwide.

12. To the horror of German elites, the S.P.D. became the largest party in Germany in 1912.

13. Nationalist leagues (the Navy League, the Army League, the Colonial League, and the Pan-German League) agitated for more assertive foreign policy, as a way of escaping internal woes.

14. A mood of crisis and pessimism about the future pervaded German elites.

C. France

1. Once the dominant power in Europe in the 18th century, France had suffered a crucial defeat in its 1870–1871 war with Germany, downgrading its power status.

2. France remained anxious about Germany, whose population overshadowed its own of 35 million, and also longed for recovery of the provinces of Alsace and Lorraine annexed by Germany.

3. France was a republic, beset by serious internal divisions among conservatives, republicans, and socialists.

4. France also had a colonial empire, through which it sought prestige to compensate for its losses in Europe.

5. France sought allies with which to oppose Germany.

D. Russia

1. Russia was an enormous multinational empire under the Romanov dynasty, spanning Europe and Asia. With a population of 164 million, it was vast in potential but still backward in development, compared with Central and Western Europe.

2. Tsar Nicholas II ruled over a traditional autocratic system that was already under strain.

3. In 1905, two disasters overtook the empire. It was defeated in the 1904–1905 Russo-Japanese War, and the Revolution of 1905 within its own borders nearly brought the regime down.

4. Russia sought to develop its potential economically and militarily, with ambitious reform plans. As the serfs had only been freed as recently as 1861, there was much ground to make up.

5. A varied revolutionary movement within Russia envisioned the overthrow of the state and the establishment of a new system, by terrorism if necessary.

6. Dissatisfied nationalities (Poles, Lithuanians, Finns, and others) saw Russia as a "prison of nations."

7. The nationalist ideology of Pan-Slavism promoted support for other Slavic nations and a leading role for Russia.

E. Austria-Hungary

1. Also a venerable old empire under the Habsburg ruling house, this multinational state of 50 million was presided over by the aged Emperor Franz Josef, who had ruled since 1848.

2. The empire consisted of twelve major ethnic groups held together by dynastic tradition and power, not nationalism, a force that Austrian leaders had feared.

3. The older empire had been reorganized into a "Dual Monarchy" of shared rule between the German-speaking Austrians and the Hungarian elites in 1867, after defeat by Prussia in 1866.

4. The demands of dissatisfied ethnic groups, underdeveloped industrialization, and anxieties as to the survival of the empire beset its leadership.

5. The Balkans were an area of special concern to the empire, both as a field of activity and potential threat.

6. Austria-Hungary's precarious position forced it into closer and closer partnership with Germany.

III. Other Countries

A. Ottoman Empire (Turkey)

1. Called the "Sick Man of Europe," its decline contrasted with its glorious past as the Islamic sultanate, ruling from North Africa to Persia.

2. Its lagging development, nationalist revolts in remaining Balkan territories, as well as the ambitions of European powers, made its future uncertain. How to deal with its expected demise was called the "Eastern Question" and occupied European diplomats.

3. In 1908, the Young Turk nationalist revolutionary movement came to power with the aim of reviving the empire.

4. Turkey came increasingly under German influence, with military advisors, railway projects, and counsel.

B. Italy

1. Italian lands were unified under the House of Savoy from 1860.

2. With a population of 36 million, Italy had ambitions for Great Power status but faced internal problems of underdevelopment and political disunity.

3. Italian nationalists still longed for territories they called *Irredenta* (unredeemed lands) at the expense of Austria-Hungary. Colonial rivalries with France also created international animosity.

C. Serbia

1. The kingdom of Serbia was a proud state that had gained independence from the Ottoman Empire.

2. Its ambition was to lead a Balkan league uniting South Slavs under Serbian patronage.

3. Russia supported Serbia and signed an alliance in 1903.

D. Japan

1. In a remarkable self-willed transformation, Japan adopted Western technology after the 1868 Meiji Restoration.

2. Determined to become an imperialist contender, Japan went to war with China in 1894 and Russia in 1904, and annexed Korea in 1910.

E. United States

1. Separated by the Atlantic Ocean, the United States did not figure prominently in European affairs.

2. Its industrial development was striking, having overtaken both Great Britain and Germany in steel production by the start of the century.

3. In military terms, its power was potential.

IV. The Balance of Power

A. The *balance of power* is the name given to the dynamic interrelation of the Great Powers.

    1. It signifies a balance among powers with none able to dominate the others as a hegemon. Other powers unite in coalitions to resist such a hegemon.

    2. Such a balance was inaugurated after the 1648 Treaty of Westphalia and the recognition of sovereign states.

    3. The Congress of Vienna of 1815 institutionalized the balance of power as a principle of harmony and conservative solidarity, under the guidance of Prince Clemens von Metternich.

    4. This system, the Concert of Europe, broke down with the Crimean War, 1854–1856, and the wars that followed.

    5. The result was now a looser and more competitive scene. Whether equilibrium could be maintained depended to a great extent on the new Germany's role.

B. A wave of "High Imperialism" from the 1880s led to a scramble for colonies, carving up Africa and Asia.

    1. Britain and France were particular colonial rivals, and Britain and Russia also mistrusted one another in Central Asia.

    2. Germany had not participated actively in this colonial competition under Bismarck, a reflection of his policy of restraint in international politics, soon to be reversed by Kaiser Wilhelm II.

C. With growing tensions in imperial contests and with a more aggressive German foreign policy from 1890, arms races resulted.

1. On the seas, Germany built the world's second largest fleet, touching off a naval arms race with the largest fleet, Britain's. At vast expense, a new generation of Dreadnought battleships was launched.

2. On land, mass armies were built up by France, Germany, and Russia. From 1890 to 1914, European armies doubled in size.

3. Hand in hand with increased numbers of men and equipment went carefully calibrated, minute planning for military operations in anticipation of the next war. Railway timetables and speed were emphasized.

Essential Reading:

John Keegan, *The First World War*, pp. 1–23.

Supplementary Reading:

Annika Mombauer, *The Origins of the First World War: Controversies and Consensus.*

Questions to Consider:

1. Was the balance of power a good thing or a bad thing? Why?

2. Could the tensions leading up to 1914 have been settled by negotiation? Why or why not?

Europe in 1914

In this lecture, entitled "Europe in 1914," we'll be setting the stage for the explosion of the First World War in 1914 by examining the state of Europe and the world at large before the cataclysm itself. We'll be examining the states that would be the major players in the opening of the war itself that were called by the very evocative name, the Great Powers; and this was always capitalized, capital G, capital P. The Great Powers, which were Great Britain, France, Germany, Austria, Hungary, and Russia, the great powers of the European continent, as well as other contenders for Great Power status making a bid for that stature. We'll examine the diplomatic history, as well as their dynamic interaction. This is summed up in a concept, which is crucial to diplomatic history: the concept of the "balance of power."

The balance of power, as concept, suggests that whenever in a multi-polar international system—that is to say, without one or two dominant players, but a multiplicity of players as a result of this phenomenon called the balance of power—one power, which makes a bid to control all the others or to displace the others, will find itself faced with a coalition opposing it of other powers. A balance of power mechanism suggests that there will always be a complicated game of balancing, of shifting coalitions, against the bid of any power to achieve total control. We'll examine, in particular, with special reference to this concept of the balance of power, the changes which were brought about in that balance of power dynamic by a new factor in European politics, the emergence of the German Empire in the late 19th century and the turmoil that this caused in the international system. We'll also examine worldwide trends of worldwide imperialism, a growing arms race on land and at sea, and also increasing international tensions, which were moving Europe after a century of general peace towards a general war by 1914.

European society, at the start of the new 20th century, is a common civilization. For all of the national differences, there were nonetheless dialogues, a sense of shared values that were part of a self-confident European civilization organized into separate nation states or multi-national empires. Europeans, for all of their national differences and their own national pride or nationalism, in many ways recognized that they shared a common worldview. This was underlined in a sense that Europeans had a right, so many of them felt, to a special role in imperialism dominating non-Western peoples. Within Western civilization, however, within the multiplicity of states and of countries and of ethnic groups, some states, those known as the Great Powers, played a dominant role in international affairs. The litmus test of a Great Power was whether it was capable of asserting its own will in international affairs without needing to seek the approval of a Great Power. Other states, which didn't fully have the status of being Great Powers in terms of international recognition, certainly aspired to such a role.

Let's consider, in turn, the Great Powers. We'll begin with the Great Power which was viewed as the conservative, status quo dominant super power of the 19th century, Great Britain. Great Britain was very clearly an industrial and commercial power, which had played an enormous role in the 19th century. It had spearheaded that complicated process called the Industrial Revolution, which had put production as well as economy on a new industrial basis.

Britain also had won for itself, over the decades and the centuries, a world empire. This World Empire on which the British proudly stated "the sun never set" was of enormous extent; by one estimate it covered some 20% of the world's entire inhabitable land surface. It included the dominions of British settlers in Canada, Australia, New Zealand, and South Africa. It also included territories like India, which was proudly claimed as the "jewel of the British Empire," and also earlier and older imperial possessions like Ireland, which was also perennial focus for unrest in Britain's own colonial backyard.

Britain's own population was 45 million, and in its island vastness, it was an empire that was dependent on trade. Britain had made itself the preeminent naval power to protect access to its overseas possessions and to secure the sea-lanes, and the British preferred, in this complicated game of the balance of power that we'll be talking more about in today's lecture, they preferred to take the stance not of direct involvement in the affairs of the continent, but rather to maintain what they proudly called "splendid isolation;" intervening in the affairs of the European continent only as necessary to preserve the balance of power. Britain's political system was a constitutional monarchy. Britain at this point had a liberal government, which was proud of the achievements of the British monarchy and the British

Empire. There was much to be proud of: a sense of preeminence in financial terms was among these factors. London was clearly the banking capital of the world. At the start of the 20th century, the British looked back upon not only a record of imperial dominance, but also a sense of investment in the status quo, a sense of being a conservative power, which wanted to preserve its preeminence among other Great Powers.

At the same time however, as we turn to examine another Great Power, British supremacy had been challenged by a brash, young contender in the game of the Great Powers, and that was Germany. The German Empire had been created recently, and it had been created by war. It had been born of the war in 1870 to 1871, when the German Kingdom of Prussia had led German armies, its allies of other German states, to victory against France, considered the hereditary enemy. As a result of this war, it was possible to establish the German Empire around Prussian leadership, a tactic that was pursued and won by the so-called Iron Chancellor, Otto von Bismarck, and the leader of Prussian politics.

Otto von Bismarck was a peerless practitioner of *Realpolitik,* a German phrase often translated in English as power politics. As the chief servant of the royal family of Prussia, the Hohenzollerns, Bismarck carefully engineered German unification around a hard core of Prussian militarism in a succession of wars against Austria in 1866, and then against France, sealing the establishment of the German Empire. This new, young Germany had become, at a stroke, in 1870 to 1871, the strongest power on the continent. It was endowed with proud Prussian militarist traditions. It had an enormous and growing population of 65 million, and its booming economy likewise made it an industrial powerhouse in a new surge of industrial revolution.

The creation of this German Empire was of such importance to international affairs, the contemporaries had to struggle with the question of how to come to terms with this new political fact. Indeed, where earlier one had had essentially a power vacuum at the center of Europe, there was this new principal, this new factor in power politics. Contemporaries at the time spoke of this unprecedented event as the "German Revolution." By calling it this, they were very clearly placing it on a par with the French Revolution at the end of the 18th century that had overturned the political order.

This, in international terms, was a fact that needed to be dealt with. The German Revolution had produced what contemporaries called, the "German Question." The German Question, which continued to haunt international politics through much of the 20th century, was essentially a way of asking what role would this new Germany play in European affairs. Would it be an anchor of European stability; or would it be a factor for instability, chaos, and perhaps war? Otto von Bismarck, an international politician of enormous sophistication, also had to deal with the German Question. He dealt with it in part by trying to calm the potential fears of other Great Powers, to insure in part that Germany wouldn't face a hostile coalition of powers balancing off against its perceived threat. He aimed to reassure the other Great Powers that Germany had only peaceful intentions. Bismarck's principal was to present Germany at all junctures as a satisfied power that had what it wanted, that was satiated, and that now after being a revolutionary factor in international politics would become a conservative in international politics.

These cautious policies, these attempts to calm the fears, potential fears, of neighbors were simply too mild a policy prescription for the young emperor—the word in German is *Kaiser*—by the name of Wilhelm II who ascended to the throne in 1888. He objected to Bismarck's attempts to calm other powers, and instead insisted on a far more energetic policy. He soon dismissed Bismarck in 1890, and set about crafting a far more assertive approach to international politics. His slogan was announced with the words, "full steam ahead."

Now, under his control nobody was really sure exactly what the course would be, but it was clear that it would be fast and it would be aggressive. A few words about this really remarkable personality of Wilhelm II would be in place here. He was, on the one hand, the descendent of a long and distinguished aristocratic line, the royal family of the House of Prussia, the family of Hohenzollern. He was also, as it turns out, the grandson of Queen Victoria of Great Britain. This speaks volumes about the interrelated kinship networks between the royal families of Europe.

But Wilhelm II distinguished himself also by many other unfortunate characteristics. He was notoriously emotionally unstable. He was given to macho posturing and extremely aggressive language. In famous newsreels of this period his figure is always very quickly to be picked out from a crowd of aristocrats because he is the one who is gesturing with wide and dramatic, very aggressive gestures, even when in engaged in making small talk with fellow aristocrats. According to historians who place a lot of store by personal psychology, Wilhelm II's physical infirmity, the fact that he was born with a withered arm as the result of a difficult birth process, according to some historians, goes some way towards explaining his posturing, his over compensation in terms of aggressive militarism, for what he perceived a physical malady that a war lord shouldn't have.

His militarism was reflected in his love of resplendent uniforms and his militaristic language that often would produce a really characteristic talent for disaster. Wilhelm II would often engage in incautious interviews with the international press, which would produce scandals that he then would have to retreat from. One problem is that this intemperate man was also surrounded by figures at court that were not very helpful in taming some of his policies. One famous case, which made clear that he was surrounded by irresponsible individuals, involved news leaking out at the start of the 20th century that at one point, when Wilhelm II had to be cheered up from one of these public relations disasters he had unleashed, some of his own generals dressed up as ballerinas and danced for him at court. One of those generals actually had a heart attack and fell dead while dancing for the Emperor dressed as a ballerina. As news of this filtered out, it was not very much calculated to reassure people that Germany's leadership was in firm and responsible hands. Wilhelm II's policies were determined, above all, to win respect and status for Germany. In his words, "Germany deserved its place in the sun." As a result, he sanctioned an aggressive foreign policy that very shortly alienated many of the Great Powers, precisely the thing that Bismarck had aimed to avoid.

Germany was a strange political creation. Though it had a parliament called the Reichstag, the empire was in fact an uneasy mix of constitutionalism and some democratic seeming elements on the one hand, and on the other hand authoritarianism, the personal rule of an unbalanced individual like Wilhelm II. German domestic politics in fact were fragmented along class, regional, and religious lines, so there was a certain volatility to German politics, which further was exacerbated by the phenomenon of rapid, very thorough, and late industrialization within Germany, which brought social disruption.

This social disruption for German conservatives and German ruling elites was summed up in the figure of one new political force that many of them feared—this was the SPD. The SPD—the initials stood for the Social Democratic Party of Germany—was a party that identified itself with the working classes. Founded in 1875, the Social Democratic Party, the SPD, adhered to Marx's ideas of a revolution overcoming capitalism and ushering in an age of worker's control. The SPD was a self-consciously revolutionary party. It was well organized and disciplined, and became a model for other socialists worldwide, including in the United States, who sought to emulate this elder brother of the international socialist movement.

To the horror of Germany's ruling elites, the SPD, in the voting in 1912, became the largest party in Germany. A sense of crisis was building from these political facts, and Germany's established elites and German nationalists sought some way in which it might be possible to escape from these domestic problems. There arose now a plethora of nationalist leagues, pressing and endorsing Wilhelm II's demand for a more aggressive foreign policy, in some cases outdoing his bellicose sentiments. These included the Navy League, the Army League, the Colonial League, and the Pan German League, arguing that all Germans living around the world needed to, together, engage in a mission of "national greatness." They all agitated for a more assertive foreign policy in part as a way of escaping this sense of internal domestic crisis. A mood of crisis and pessimism about the future haunted German elites, and many historians argue affected the decisions made at the time of the outbreak of the Second [sic First] World War.

Let's turn next to examine the case of what had been a dominant super power, France. France had been the super power of Europe in the 18th century, but had suffered a crucial defeat later in the 19th century in its war against Prussia in 1870–1871. Its defeat had led not only to a crisis of political moral within France itself, but also internationally had tended to downgrade the power status of France. After that war, France remained anxious about its new neighbor, Germany. The German Problem, or the German Question, was existential for France. France's own population of about 35 million was overshadowed by Germany's larger population. Many French politicians also longed for the recovery of the lost provinces of Alsace and Lorraine, with many French speakers annexed by

Germany after the French defeat in the Franco Prussian War. France itself was a republic, beset nonetheless by serious internal divisions between different kinds of political orientations: conservatives, republicans, and socialists. France also had a colonial empire where it sought in part to compensate for the loss of its prestige in Europe. And, in almost a textbook case of the operation of the balance of power, a weakened France sought allies, which might help it to oppose a future German threat.

We'll turn to next to examine the enigmatic and huge, outsized Great Power of the Russian Empire. Russia, to the east, was an enormous and, in many ways, mysterious empire ruled by the Romanov dynasty spanning two continents, Europe as well as Asia. With a huge population of 164 million, as well as vast natural resources, the Russian Empire was vast in potential, but still at present backward in terms of its industrial development compared to Central or Western Europe. It was ruled over not by constitutional or democratic system, but rather by a tsar, an emperor, Nicholas II, who ruled over a traditional, autocratic system that was already under stain.

Though certain accommodations had been made to introduce some elements of constitutionalism or more democratic government, the tsar, Nicholas II, took very seriously his own role as the personal ruler of these lands. In particular, his reign was marked by two disasters, which had overtaken the Russian Empire at the start of the 20th century in 1905. Russia had been defeated in the 1904–1905 Russo-Japanese War, something that was unheard of: a defeat by non-European power of a European Great Power. As a result of this humiliation and the crisis of that war in 1905, Russia had been wracked by a revolution, the Revolution of 1905, which very nearly brought the regime down within Russia itself.

In the years that followed, Russia sought to develop its vast potential, both economically and militarily, with ambitious reform programs, but there was much ground to make up. The Russian peasantry, the serfs, had only been freed in 1861, and it lagged behind in agricultural as well as industrial development. In part because of the repressiveness of Russia's political authorities, which tended to make revolutionaries out of people who otherwise might have been reformers, a varied revolutionary movement within Russia grew up and envisioned the overthrow of the state and the establishment of new system by terrorism, if necessary. On the peripheries of this Russian dominated empire, there were also many dissatisfied nationalities that were not Russian. These included the Poles, Lithuanians, Latvians, Estonians, Finns, and others who denounced Russia not as a glorious multinational empire, but rather as a prison of nations denying them their longed after national independence. Paradoxically, the same system of the tsarist empire presented itself outside, with a nationalist ideology of Pan-Slavism, as the patron of other Slavic nationalities, and taking a leading role in the liberation of Slavic peoples not under Russian rule.

The other traditional empire that played a Great Power role was Austria-Hungary. It was a venerable old empire under the Habsburg ruling house. This multinational state of 50 million was presided over by the aged Emperor Franz Josef from his capital in Vienna. He had ruled since 1848, and had become so intensely identified with Austro-Hungarian legitimacy that many grew to worry that his passing with time might not undermine the empire's own existence. The empire consisted of twelve major ethnic groups, held together by dynastic tradition and power, not by unified nationalism, a force that Austrian leaders, on the contrary, feared. The older empire had been reorganized into the so-called "Dual Monarchy" of shared rule between the German-speaking Austrians and the Hungarian elites in 1867, after the Habsburg Empire had been defeated by Bismarck's Prussia in 1866. Henceforth, it would be known as the Austro-Hungarian Empire. The demands of dissatisfied ethnic groups, the challenges of underdeveloped industrialization, and anxieties for the survival of the empire beset its leadership. Geographically, the Balkans was an area of special concern to the empire to the south, both as a field of activity for themselves, as well as potential threat of nationalism to the rule. Austria-Hungary's precarious position, its uncertain chances for survival, tended to force it into closer and closer partnership with Imperial Germany.

Other powers that were not of Great Power status, but nonetheless figured, included the Ottoman Empire or Turkey. This was often called the "Sick Man of Europe," because of its steady geopolitical decline, which contrasted in such dramatic terms with its glorious past as the Islamic sultanate, stretching from North Africa to Persia in the east. Ottoman Turkey's lagging development, nationalist revolts in few remaining Balkan territories, and ambitions of European powers to cover up its imperial holdings made its future especially uncertain. How to deal with its expected demise was called by European politicians the "Eastern Question"—how very polite—and, in fact, occupied European diplomats intensely. In a last ditch effort to save what remained of the Ottoman Empire, in 1908 a so-called "Young Turk" nationalist revolutionary movement came to power with the aim of reviving the empire. Turkey came increasingly under German influence, with military advisors, railway projects, and counsel from that patron power.

Another contender for Great Power status was Italy. Italian lands had been unified late, as Germany would later be, under the House of Savoy from 1860. With a population of 36 million, thus smaller than the other Great Powers, Italy had intense ambitions for Great Power status, but within faced internal problems of underdevelopment and political disunity. Italian nationalists also were keenly aware the territories that they still claimed, and they called them the *Irredenta*, or unredeemed lands, remained outside of Italy's geographic scope; Austria-Hungary held these territories, and this was a source of friction of between the powers. Colonial rivalries with France also created international animosity in Italian foreign relations.

Most certainly a Great Power, but a regional power was the kingdom of Serbia in the Balkans. The kingdom of Serbia was a proud Balkan state, which had fought for and gained independence from Ottoman rule over the course of the 19th century, but its ambitions were even larger. They were to lead, someday, a Balkan league uniting South Slavs under Serbian patronage. And, they enjoyed in this aim the support of Russia, a Slavic Great Power to the east, a big brother that had signed an alliance in 1903 in support of its aims.

There were also two remarkable powers that were bidding for Great Power status that were not European, and this what made them special. One of them was Japan. In a truly remarkable, self-willed transformation from within, Japan had adopted Western technology and aspects of political organization after the 1868 so-called Meiji Restoration. Determined to imitate the Europeans in their successes, Japan also wanted to become an imperialist contender in the Pacific; and thus it went to war with China in 1894; with Russia in 1904, and beat that Great Power of Europe; and annexed Korea in 1910, becoming an imperialist Great Power.

The final case of a Great Power emerging on to the scene was the United States. Separated by the Atlantic Ocean from European affairs, the United States did not figure prominently in Great Power politics; nonetheless, keen observers anticipated a future for it of significant proportions. Its industrial development was striking, in that by the start of the 20th century it had overtaken both Great Britain and Germany in steel production, a key measure of industrialization. In military terms, while its army was small, its navy was growing; its potential power was quite significant.

We'll close with some observations about the notion of the balance of power at work in international relations. The "balance of power" is the name given to that dynamic interrelation and interplay of the Great Powers. The concept signifies a balance between powers with no one power capable of totally dominating the others. If it were capable of doing so, it would have attained the status of, what's called in political science or political philosophy, hegemon, with hegemonic or total power. The balance of power concept suggests that whenever a contender for hegemonic power arises, all other powers will unite in coalitions to resist such a hegemon. The operation of the balance of power is a long-standing factor in European politics. It was inaugurated after the 1648 Treaty of Westphalia ended the titanic struggle of the Thirty Years War in Europe. The 1648 Treaty of Westphalia crafted the balance of power not by design, but simply by recognizing sovereign states as political actors. The Congress of Vienna of 1815, which brought to end the Napoleonic wars, by contrast formally institutionalized the idea of the balance of power as a principle of harmony, and conservative solidarity under the guidance of the masterful Austrian diplomat Prince Clemens von Metternich. The notion was that the balance of power was a good that had to be preserved through periodic conferences of the Great Powers that would avoid wars but instead settle problems among themselves, and would institutionalize in a peaceful way the balance of power.

This system, which was called by the really marvelously evocative name of the "Concert of Europe," that's to say the Great Powers acting in concert, lasted for decades and insured nearly a century without larger general wars in Europe. But it had started to break down in the course of the 19th century, especially with the Crimean War 1854 to 1856, which pitted the Great Powers of Great Britain and France against Russia. And other wars obviously followed, including those of Bismarck and the wars of German unification.

Thus, at the end of the 19th century and the start of the 20th century, the result was now a more loose and competitive scene in international politics. Whether equilibrium could be maintained through Great Power politics and the balance of power would depend to a great extent, as we've already suggested, on the role of the new Germany.

Other factors in international politics were also imperialism. A wave of high imperialism from the 1880s had led to a frantic scramble for colonies, carving up Africa and Asia, with even smaller powers like Belgium getting involved in the act. The key players here were Britain and France, who were particular colonial rivals. Britain was also worried about Russian's intentions in Central Asia. Germany, by contrast—and this irked Wilhelm II—had not participated actively in this colonial scramble because of Bismarck's policy of abstention. Kaiser Wilhelm II would soon remove this restraint, and the result would be an increasing arms race in international politics, with growing tensions in imperialism, as well as a more aggressive German foreign policy from 1890.

Arms races resulted on land as well as at sea. On the seas, Germany, under Wilhelm II's aggressive policy, built the world's second largest fleet, touching off a naval arms race with the world's largest fleet, Britain's. A vast expense of a new generation of so-called "Dreadnought" battleships was launched, inaugurating a whole new stage of naval competition. On land, meanwhile, mass armies were built up by France, Germany, and Russia from 1890–1914; European armies had doubled in size. Hand-in-hand with increased numbers of men and equipment went increasingly carefully calibrated minute planning for military operations at the start of the war. Railway timetables and speed were emphasized, as the European Great Powers prepared for an apocalyptic conflict. Many contemporaries recognized this was potentially steering towards a general war, and the crisis in politics as well as in thought and culture that accompanied this mood of anticipation and anxiety, we'll examine in our next lecture.

Lecture Three

Towards Crisis in Politics and Culture

Scope:

This lecture probes the deeper forces pushing a previously coherent European civilization toward crisis and world war. We examine first the distinctive ideas and mindsets of the day and then turn to the premonitions noted by insightful contemporaries of coming disaster. In politics, a new orientation toward public opinion and the role of the masses was strengthened. Social Darwinist celebrations of the "survival of the fittest" led to views of war as a form of hygiene. Even trends in socialist thought took on apocalyptic tendencies in expectation of total social upheaval. Last, we turn to examine the illusions of war and peace: misconceptions about the nature of the conflict to come, its alleged promises of glory and transcendence, and heroes "home by Christmas."

Outline

I. Ideas and Mindsets

    A. Progress

        1. European cultural confidence was based on the prized notion of progress.

        2. Enormous visible progress had taken place in the sciences, medicine, and industry.

        3. A second wave of industrial advance from 1871, called the Second Industrial Revolution, brought accelerating change.

        4. Science also lent prestige to Social Darwinist thought and "scientific" racism, undergirding imperialist domination of non-Western peoples.

        5. A proud symbol of technological progress that turned into a troubling portent was the RMS *Titanic*, a ship, which, as a tremendous technical accomplishment, seemed invulnerable, scorning the elements until it hit an iceberg and sank in 1912 with more than 1,500 killed. This example of technology running ahead of understanding would be repeated in World War I.

B. Liberalism

    1. An ideology that identified itself with progress was classical liberalism, with origins in the Enlightenment and strongly represented in the middle classes.

    2. Liberalism was a faith in individual freedom and individualism, constitutional restraints on a limited state, capitalism and free trade, with progress growing out of competition in the marketplace of ideas and economics.

C. Nationalism

    1. An extremely important ideology, nationalism had often turned from its revolutionary and liberal origins to forms that were chauvinistic.

    2. Originally a message of liberation, it was used by nation-states to reinforce governmental legitimacy.

    3. In places where "submerged peoples" clamored for self-determination, nationalism could be an explosive force, especially in multinational empires like Russia and Austria-Hungary.

    4. By the later 19th century, notions of hierarchies of peoples, of "rising" and "declining" races were commonplace.

D. Conservatism

    1. Resisting liberal ideologies, but incorporating nationalist ideas when they could, some European regimes and parties championed conservatism.

    2. Whereas in Britain this political development took the form of evolutionary conservatism that was open to change, on the continent, meanwhile, aristocratic privilege and caste took pride of place in the empires.

E. Socialism

    1. Karl Marx (1818–1883) had promulgated a "scientific socialism," promising an international workers' revolution, the dictatorship of the proletariat, abolition of private property, and a classless utopia to follow.

    2. Especially in Germany, a powerful and disciplined Social Democratic movement grew up.

3. Socialism could be either feared or hoped for. The *Internationale*, the anthem of the movement, foretold an imminent "final battle."

II. Politics

    A. The effect of politics on the masses bears some consideration.

        1. Since the French Revolution of 1789, politics implied appeals to the masses for legitimacy, even if only on the level of rhetoric.

        2. Increased participation of larger groups in politics transformed its dynamics.

    B. Such participation could lead to acceptance of conflict.

        1. The ideologies of liberalism, nationalism, conservatism, and even socialism could all implicitly be used to justify acceptance of competition or conflict.

        2. The feared opposite of vigorous competition was decline and degeneration, a besetting anxiety of the age.

        3. This anxiety affected views of war.

    C. Such views bring us to the topic of militarism.

        1. War was often seen as a test of national identity and worth.

        2. Militarism, defined as the supremacy of the armed forces' code of virtues over that of civilian society, was visible in many European countries, but especially identified with Germany and its Prussian elite, including Kaiser Wilhelm II.

            a. Historians speak of a feudalization and brutalization of the German middle classes, as they imitated the Junker officer aristocracy.

            b. German students prized dueling scars.

            c. The respect shown to reserve officers emphasized the status of the German military.

            d. Pressure groups and nationalist leagues demanded aggressive foreign policy and increased military expenditures.

      e. The person of Kaiser Wilhelm II, with his love of uniforms, parades, and aggressive rhetoric, symbolized this militaristic tendency best.

      f. Not all Germans subscribed to these militarist values.

  D. To some, war appeared as a way out of political crisis or social stalemate.

III. Culture

  A. Social Darwinism

    1. Disturbing trends in the culture included Social Darwinism, which praised the "survival of the fittest" and the "struggle for survival."

    2. Some saw war as a form of social hygiene, condemning peace as enervating.

  B. Misconceptions on the Nature of Modern War

    1. War was often thought of as short, fast, and glorious. Absurdly romanticized popular depictions seconded this view.

    2. At the same time, there were many hints that the future war would in fact take on a very different visage.

    3. The Russo-Japanese War of 1904–1905 and the American Civil War had seen trenches, the devastating impact of modern military technologies, and facets of total war.

    4. Only racist condescension obscured the dreadful lessons of imperial conquests of non-European peoples. In the 1898 Battle of Omdurman, British forces had annihilated a far larger Sudanese force with Maxim guns.

    5. It was also expected that war could be restrained. The Geneva Conventions of 1864 and 1906 and the Hague Conventions of 1899 and 1907 outlined rules for "civilized warfare," including protecting civilians and prisoners and banning some new weapons like poison gas.

  C. Celebrations and Fears

    1. In European popular culture, an extensive speculative literature and pulp fiction forecast "the next war."

2. In Italy, the Futurist movement's 1910 manifesto praised technology, speed, danger, and war as escapes from a boring, orderly world.

3. In Paris in 1913, Stravinsky's ballet *Rite of Spring* shocked the public with its novelty and its startling theme of human sacrifice.

4. Challenging the order and respectability of 19th-century society, the life-philosophy of Friedrich Nietzsche (1844–1900) celebrated strength, the will to power, moral adventure "beyond good and evil," toward the goal of evolving the superman, the *Übermensch*.

5. In Germany, the *Wandervogel* movement of back-to-nature hikers spearheaded generational revolt and longed for a world remade by idealism.

IV. Readying for War

    A. According to the eminent military historian John Keegan, turn-of-the-century Europe was "pregnant with war."

    B. Military planning was increasingly important.

        1. In its 1870–1871 victory over France, the Prussian army had seemingly demonstrated the key to military success: universal conscription, large reserves, and scientific precision in planning to achieve speedy mobilization.

        2. As a result, military planning in all the Great Powers grew ever more detailed, dominated by railroad timetables. Mobilization increasingly implied war, as, once started, plans had to unfold.

        3. If speed was crucial, it underlined the importance of putting the maximum force into the first blow.

        4. The German army's secret Schlieffen Plan, sought to deal with the geopolitical problem of Germany's exposed position and the potential for war on two fronts.

        5. The plan was crafted by General Alfred von Schlieffen, chief of the German general staff from 1891–1905.

6. Its aim was to knock out France in 42 days by a sweeping movement of armies through neutral Belgium and Holland, plunging through northern France, to encircle French armies and Paris. Afterward, German armies would turn to face the slower Russian foe.

7. Its disregard for political and diplomatic realities made it a clear example of militaristic abstraction.

8. The French Plan XVII projected a victorious reconquest of the lost provinces of Alsace and Lorraine.

9. Russian plans for the attack on Germany were prepared.

C. All of this planning was given further impetus by the cult of the offensive.

1. In a counterpoint to military planning and technocratic organization was the emphasis on the spirit of attack, called the cult of the offensive.

2. Generals and officers argued that fiercely dedicated soldiers could overrun their enemies even against greater odds.

3. Training emphasized bayonet drill and attack.

4. In the French case, the crucial quality of spirit was called "*élan vital*" and implied all-out extreme attack, to compensate for France's smaller population.

5. Once the largest nation in Europe, France by 1914 could field only 60 percent of German potential manpower.

6. The young officer Charles de Gaulle proclaimed in 1913, "Everywhere, always, one should have a single idea: to advance."

Essential Reading:

Modris Eksteins, *Rites of Spring: The Great War and the Birth of the Modern Age*, pp. 1–54.

Supplementary Reading:

John Keegan, *The First World War*, pp. 24–47.

Questions to Consider:

1. What forces worked against a readiness for war in Europe?

2. Which aspect of European culture was most problematic and troubling before 1914?

Lecture Three—Transcript
Towards Crisis in Politics and Culture

In this lecture, we'll be examining some of the deeper forces that were pushing a previously coherent European civilization towards crisis and ultimately world war. We'll examine first of all the distinctive ideas and mindsets of the day. We'll turn then to examine politics in which a new orientation towards public opinion—the participation of masses in politics, and the role of those masses—was strengthened. We'll examine also disturbing sets of ideas like social Darwinist celebrations of the "survival of the fittest" that produced views of war not as a tragedy, but rather as form of hygiene for civilization. Even trends in socialist thought, which otherwise rejected the disaster of war, could take on apocalyptic tendencies in expectation of the final, total revolution that would lead to the coming of a blessed state without exploitation. Last, we'll turn to examine some of the illusions of war and peace, misconceptions about the nature of the conflict to come, and its alleged promises of glory and transcendence and heroism.

One of the key ideas that was of enormous significance in a shared European civilization—for all of its national difference—was a certain confidence in the idea of progress. European cultural confidence presented progress as a very crown to the achievements, the self-evident superiority, so Europeans claimed, of their civilization. Indeed, in the process of reckoning up examples of this progress there clearly had been enormous visible gains in the field of the sciences, medicine, and obviously in terms of industry and productivity. If anything, these changes—this progress as it was viewed—was speeding up. A second wave of industrial advance from 1871 called the Second Industrial Revolution was bringing accelerating change and bringing new industrial materials; so that, for instance, if the First Industrial Revolution had been to great extent based on coal, the Second Industrial Revolution already was focusing on the internal combustion engine, was based on chemicals and recognizably more modern forms of technology. Historians would probably be quick to point that 1871 is a suspiciously exact date for the beginning of the Second Industrial Revolution. There was a moment here that we want to simply bring into focus. Why 1871, for the beginning of a new wave of industrial? The date corresponds to the founding of a German Empire in 1871, under

Prussian leadership that we've discussed in earlier lectures. Very clearly, Germany was playing a leading role in this second wave of industrialization. The First Industrial Revolution, as it's often called, from the 18th century had been based in Great Britain, which had taken the leading role. Now it seemed to some, a worrying factor that Germany was taking the lead.

Science also lent prestige to Social Darwinist thought and the notion of scientific racism, that's to say racism claiming to have the imprimatur of science, all of which under girded imperialist domination of non-Western peoples by—so it was alleged—giving them a claim to rule of other races. A proud symbol of technological progress, which turned into a troubling portent for things to come, was the case of the great and proud transatlantic liner, the *Titanic*. It was seen at its time as a tremendous technical accomplishment, which seemed to contemporaries almost invulnerable, able to scorn the elements. It was precisely this hubris about its invulnerability that let it to hit an iceberg and to sink in 1912 with more than 1,500 passengers killed. This example, from just before the outbreak of the First World War, of technology and confidence in the technology running ahead of understanding of its limitations or its liabilities, in an uncanny way would be repeated many times in World War I.

Among the distinctive ideas that were associated with progress and its promise was the key concept or ideology of liberalism. Liberalism was a self-confident, which identified its ideas and its prescriptions with the promise of progress. Also called "classical liberalism," this ideology had its origins in the Enlightenment thought of the 18th century, and strongly represented in the European middle classes, who not coincidentally identified themselves with the very progress of the enlightened and of liberalism. Classical liberalism can be summed up as a faith in personal freedom and individualism bringing progress. Many prescriptions about politics and society and economics flowed for classical liberals from this faith in the individual. These included constitutional restraints to produce a limited state, so that the government would have to a give a sphere or scope for individual freedoms and the free unfolding of one's personality and one's talents. In the economic realm, capitalism and free trade, the maximally unimpeded traffic of goods and of ideas and of finance, was held up as bringing the greatest common good for all. Progress, it was judged, tended to grow out of a process of competition in the marketplace of economics, as well as ideas. The best ideas would win out as a result of vigorous debate and argument.

Another tremendously important ideology, at first closely identified with liberalism, was known as "nationalism." Nationalism, in spite of many predictions of its upcoming demise, is still very much with us today in our own times, and shows every sign of growing stronger. It had undergone a process of evolution. Nationalism had turned from its revolutionary and liberal origins at the start of the 19th century to forms that increasingly could be chauvinistic and narrow. Turning away from its message of universal liberation, it could often be used by nation-states and government elites to reinforce the legitimacy of their own authority and their own rule.

Nonetheless, nationalism, even at the start of the 20th century, still had the potential to be a revolutionary force, especially in places where so-called "submerged peoples" clamored for self-determination. Multinational empires like Russia and Austria-Hungary certainly had many different ethnic groups that didn't feel that they were represented by the authorities or by the government elites, and in such places nationalism as a set of ideas and as a prescription for action could be an explosive force. And it was truly feared by the rulers of those multiethnic empires precisely for that reason. One needs to think one's way into a mindset or worldview in this period in which nationalism seemed to be a self-evident, almost organically given form of identity. By the later nineteenth century, there were remarkably current notions of hierarchies of peoples. It was simply judged natural at the time that one could distinguish between peoples in terms of their achievements, and to, as it were, categorize or rate their civilizational achievements. These notions of hierarchies of people also carried with it an undertone or a subtext that could be quite threatening, depending on one's position in these hierarchies of peoples. The notion of there being peoples who were rising and growing in strength and vitality, and other races that were declining or headed for weakness and enervation or maybe even extinction, was commonplace. One most definitely, in this period of nationalism, wanted to belong to the rising peoples rather than those on their way out.

In contrast to liberal ideologies, but in vigorous debate with them in a philosophical dialogue, was another ideology called "conservatism," which had arisen in part in response in challenges of these bold new liberal ideas. Conservatives resisted liberal ideologies, but over time they had started to incorporate nationalist ideas when they could, and in the process of the 19th century they had imagined to diffuse some of the revolutionary potential of nationalism by turning nationalism into a support for their own regime or their party. Now clearly, neither liberals nor conservatives were monolithic groups who all felt the same thing. In terms of conservatism, there were some really remarkable contrasts. In Britain, conservatism as an ideology took a specific form later called "evolutionary conservatism," with a notion that a society should be open to change, and that indeed, as the famous formula went, change was the very principle of preservation. On the continent, by contrast, conservatives instead saw themselves as on the defensive, protecting aristocratic privilege and caste, especially if they belonged to multinational empires threatened by nationalist ideas.

We need to add to this dynamic and often exciting mix of philosophical stances a stance, which was self-consciously revolutionary, and remains so; that was "socialism." Karl Marx, a socialist thinker from Germany, had promulgated a new kind of socialism, which he announced was to overtake and improve upon all of the earlier utopian socialisms that had promulgated in the course of the 19th century. His version of scientific socialism, which he announced at the middle of the 19th century, promised a scientific program for achieving an international workers' revolution, which would overthrow capitalism and its system of exploitation, establish the dictatorship of the proletariat, the abolition of private property, and a classless utopia free of exploitation, with the fullest human development for all said to follow.

As we've already commented in an earlier lecture, especially in Germany, this message had tremendous force. A powerful and disciplined Social Democratic movement grew up in order to follow these prescriptions for scientific socialism. Socialism in this period was seen as most definitely a fact in politics, whether one feared or hoped for. Socialists lived in the expectation that they were on the right side of history, and that it is was moving in the direction that Marx had prescribed, one that was leading to a climax of historical proportions. And this was made very clear in the anthem of their movement. The nationalists had their national anthems; the socialists, by contrast, had their international anthem, known as the *Internationale*. This anthem of the movement foretold in ringing tones the imminent "final battle" that would lead to a comprehensive human liberation under the banner of socialism.

We need to turn next to examine the implications that these ideas would have for politics, politics in a time of change, a time of change in which the masses needed to be incorporated. Since the French Revolution of 1789, politics had been fundamentally changed. Politics had now come to imply the need for all regimes to appeal to the masses for legitimacy, to appeal to the broader population even if only on the level of rhetoric. Even personal autocracies, like that of the Russian Empire or of Imperial Germany, nonetheless tried to at least create the impression of popular monarchist fervor in support of their regime. Now, it's obvious that this new infusion of the masses into politics—the increased participation of larger groups and the need to appeal to them—transformed the dynamics of politics, made populist appeals and dynamism certainly more desirable, and as we'll be seeing shortly, also could lead to an increased acceptance of conflict.

The ideologies of liberalism, nationalism, conservatism, and even socialism that we've outlined just so very briefly now, could all implicitly be used to justify at least some measure of the acceptance of competition or conflict as producing progress. One reason for this was, well, when one considered what the opposite alternative was: the feared opposite of vigorous competition or conflict was seen by many people not as state of universal peace but instead, in line with thinking in terms of hierarchies of rising or declining race, as degeneration, de-civilization. A besetting anxiety of the age was precisely this, that some vitality, some dynamism would be lost. This in turn would affect views of war, even on the part of liberals who hoped certainly that progress would be won through competition in the marketplace, peacefully, and who denounced war as a destructive factor in politics, nonetheless they had endorsed competition. The socialists, as we've already seen, even as they looked forward to the day when the fundamental political reordering of the world would take place in line with their ideas, nonetheless looked forward to an explosive revolution—a conflict certainly—in order to bring this about.

As such ideas and acceptance of conflicts changed views of war, we need to speak about another allied phenomenon, that of "militarism." War was often seen, at the close of the 19th century and the start of the 20th century, not exclusively in terms of being a man-made tragedy, but often as something else in addition, as a test of national identity, whether people had the requisite vitality that assured their status as a rising race, as a test of national worth and cohesion. Militarism, one probably shouldn't consider a full-fledged ideology in the sense that nationalism or liberalism or conservatism were; rather, militarism simply expressed the notion that values of the armed forces, their code of virtues of obedience, of duty, of command, of hierarchy, were supreme over that of civilian society, and as part and parcel of the growing arms races, as a concomitant of the growing tension in Europe. Militarism could be seen in many European countries, not always dominant, but nonetheless as an option socially, nonetheless. Militarism was, however, especially identified with one country where this word was, to many, not a feature to be avoided but, on the contrary, was seen as good and an old part of German tradition, and that was Germany.

Germany, especially in its Prussian elite, seemed a very embodiment of the values of militarism, and there was no better embodiment of this code of values than Kaiser Wilhelm II. Historians who examine Germany have spoken of a process almost of re-feudalization taking in the place in the course of the later 19th century. They sometimes speak of a process of brutalization of the German middle classes; what they mean by this is German middle classes who otherwise would have been carriers of liberal ideas often tended, as a result of the ideas of militarism, to try to imitate the old established officer aristocracies of Prussian military tradition and German military tradition. These older office aristocracies in the case of Prussia were known as the *Junkers*. The middle classes valued their style and tried when they were able to imitate their older traditional feudal ways.

To give just but one very vivid example, German university students in those days often would appear—and then for the rest of their lives would appear—with faces that were cross hatched and marked with dueling scars, long scars that would run from one side of the face to the other. This was something that they didn't see as a disfigurement, but, on the contrary, were proud of. It was a sign that they were sharing in medieval tradition of dueling, that they were men of honor and that they were capable of engaging in this military ritual. Another example that made clear the popularity of these militarist ideas in large segments of German society was the tremendous respect that was shown to reserve officers whose wearing of uniforms—whether in the classroom if they were professors or on special occasions—emphasized the status and the respect that the German military was accorded.

At the same time, as we've already discussed in earlier lectures, nationalist pressure groups and leagues like the Army League, the Navy League, or the Colonial League all demanded aggressive foreign policy, and in fact criticized even the Kaiser's government for not doing enough in that regard, and also clamored for increased military expenditures in a cycle of militarism. As we've already adverted, the person of Kaiser Wilhelm II was the perfect embodiment of these trends. Many people felt at the time that he somehow was in tune with the spirit of the age; his love of uniforms, parades, and aggressive rhetoric and militarism seemed to symbolize precisely this. Now, it needs, nonetheless, to be pointed out that not all Germans subscribed to these militarist values. This was not a monolithic emotion seizing an entire nation, and in fact, in particular, the Social Democrats, out of their political convictions, criticized militarism as unhealthy, as a diversion from a real program of fundamental political reform. At the same time, however, especially among Germany's elites—and the same was true in some other countries as well—war could appear to some as an escape, a way out of political crisis or social stalemate in order to recover dynamism and vitality.

We need to turn to examine the question of how culture played in this volatile mix of ideas. In this context we need to in particular focus on a disturbing trend which was not the monopoly of any one country, but on the contrary, the closer one looks at sources from the late 19th century, the more one sees it throughout western civilization, a trend called Social Darwinism. Social Darwinism was the use of Charles Darwin's ideas about evolution and about how nature moved through an evolutionary progress, but instead turned into a political agenda, a political agenda that dealt with humanity and with societies. Social Darwinism used Darwin's ideas to praise the "survival of the fittest" and the "struggle for survival" among individuals and nations. Some Social Darwinists celebrated war, seeing it as a form of social hygiene, which did away with the confining claustrophobia of peacetime society; it condemned peace as enervating and argued that war was a necessary test.

The Social Darwinists represented simply the most extreme of these celebrations of war. We want to examine some of the misconceptions about the nation of modern war that were unfortunately quite common in societies at the turn of the century. War in popular culture was often thought of as likely to be short, fast, and glorious. There were absurdly romanticized popular depictions in novels, in literature, and in journalism, which seconded these ideas. They praised clean death on the battlefield, heroism an acid test of bravery.

At the same time, however, there certainly were many hints that the future war in the 20th century would in fact take on a very different aspect from these idealized depictions. Even though historians sometimes emphasize the delusions about what the true nature of war would be like, it needs to be said that a whole number of generals—in fact, at the time military professionals—had begun to suspect for particular reasons that future war, in fact, would not take on these lines, but rather be quite different.

Some of these lessons were slow to percolate. Instances that were especially suggestive included the Russo-Japanese War of 1904 and 1905 or, more remotely, the American Civil War. Both of these increasingly industrialized forms of conflict had seen phenomenon that would be once again evident in the First World War: the battle in the trenches, the devastating impact of modern military technologies, and at least aspects of this phenomenon of total war that we earlier had introduced. In fact, one could even expand this discussion further to mention that the devastating toll which imperial conquests—the scramble for colonies in Africa or Asia—had taken on native peoples had already suggested just how destructive warfare and modern weapons could be. But only racist condescension towards those native victims of European imperialism obscured the dreadful lessons of the imperial conquests of non-European peoples.

A key moment, which disturbed even the conquerors, came in the 1898 when British forces at the battle of Omdurman in Sudan had annihilated a far larger and extremely well motivated Sudanese force by using Maxim guns, a form of a machine gun. In touching naiveté, Europeans at the time calmed themselves that Europeans would not use machine guns against fellow Europeans because this intended to be only a weapon for use against non-Western masses; and they would be dreadfully wrong, as events would show. It was also expected optimistically that war might be restrained. In fact, the notion of "civilized warfare," an ironic phrase, spoke to these hopes. The Geneva Conventions which had been negotiated in 1864 and 1906 and the Hague Conventions of 1899 and 1907 all represented an attempt to outline rules for what was called civilized warfare, including protections civilians and prisoners, the banning of some new weapons like poison gas; all imperfect, the treaties, but nonetheless attempts to somehow reign in the destructive potential of war itself. Nonetheless, war was the object of both celebrations and fears in European culture.

In European popular culture, in extensive speculative literature—today we'd call this science fiction or pulp fiction—many novels forecast or considered what the next war might be like. Some of them foretold carnage on a scale which might at least approach the reality that later transpired. But other movements in terms of culture, art, and intellectual life instead stressed an irrational celebration of war. In Italy, in a very famous case, a movement that called itself the "Futurists," in 1910 had quite deliberately shocked the world with a manifesto, a manifesto of values that included a celebration of war. The Futurist manifesto praised technology, speed, danger, and war as an escape from a boring, orderly world. They argued that museums should be burned down, that old statues were infinitely boring compared to the glory of a new racing car with all of its technology and with all of its aggressive power. They saw war as example to fulfill some of their ideas.

The year before the outbreak of the First World War also brought another tremendously significant cultural event in Paris in 1913, Stravinsky's ballet *The Rite of Spring*, a willfully primitivist and energetic ballet shocked the public with its novelty, its newness, and its theme matter which, after all, was that of a human sacrifice, anticipating, in uncanny ways, the vaster human sacrifice that was about to take place in European society.

There were earlier philosophical ideas that could be drawn upon as well in this irrationalist celebration. The life-philosophy of the German philosopher Friedrich Nietzsche had challenged the order and respectability of 19th century middle class society and many ideas of liberalism as well. Nietzsche had celebrated strength, the